# LOVE

# TO

# DANCE!

# MY FAVORITE KINDS OF DANCE ARE:

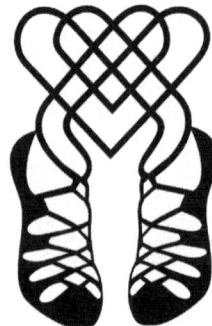

_____

_____

_____

_____

4

# DANCE

## COLORING & ACTIVITY BOOK

## MY NAME IS:

_____

## I STUDY DANCE AT:

_____

_____

Coloring, Reference & Activity pages for
Ballet, Tap, Jazz, Breakdance, Modern and Irish Dance
ISBN 978-1-7355696-8-0
Published by Krysta Bernhardt Publishing © 2024

# MY DANCE GOALS:

_____

_____

_____

_____

_____

_____

_____

_____

_____

2

If you can talk,
you can sing.
If you can walk,
you can dance.

# SOME BALLET TERMS:

## BARRE:

The railing a dancer uses for balance for exercises done at the beginning of every Ballet class.

## PLIÉ:

"To bend". Bending of the knees to help stretch the joints, muscles and tendons and make them soft and bendable.

## DEMI PLIÉ:

"Small Bend". A small knee bend that bends the knees as far as possible while keeping the heels on the ground.

## GRANDE PLIÉ:

"Big Bend". A deep knee bend deep, so that in all foot positions, except the second, the heels rise off the floor.

## RELEVÉ:

"To rise". Rising to the balls of the feet (or later the toes) from the flat foot.

## BATTEMENT TENDU:

"To stretch". An exercise that involves extending one leg from a closed position to an open position while pointing the foot and keeping the foot in contact with the floor.

## EN CROIX:

"In a cross". Barre exercise are often done this way (to the front, side and back).

# PORT DE BRAS:

"Carriage of the arms". Describes the movement of the arms in Ballet.

# RONDE DE JAMBE

"Circle of the leg". A circular leg movement. Ronds de jambe are used as an exercise at the barre and in the centre. They can be done starting to the front to the front (en dehors) and starting to the back (en dedans).

# EN FACE:

"Facing Front". When the dancer faces their body toward the front of the room (mirrors) or the audience.

# DEVANT:

"Front". Facing or moving to the front during an exercise or step.

# DERRIERE:

"Behind or back". Facing or moving to the back during an exercise or step.

# REVERANCE:

"To show reverance". The last exercise of a ballet class, where dancers pay respect to and acknowledge the teacher. It is also a bow or curtsy after a performance. It usually includes bows (for men), curtsies (for women) and ports de bras. It is a way of celebrating Ballet's traditions of elegance and respect.

# WHAT OTHER BALLET TERMS DO YOU KNOW AND USE? WRITE THEM HERE:

# DANCERS DON'T NEED WINGS TO FLY!

I ♥
BALLET

12

13

# Without dance what is the pointe?

# Life
## without
# Ballet
# is pointless!

# POSITIONS OF THE FEET
## (LEFT)

First Position

Second Position

Third Position

Fourth
Position

Fifth Position

# POSITIONS OF THE FEET
## (RIGHT)

First Position

Second Position

Third Position

Fourth Position

Fifth Position

17

# CONNECT THE TERM ON THE LEFT PAGE TO THE CORRECT FOOT POSITION ON THE RIGHT PAGE:

First Position

Fourth
Position
Left foot front)

Third Position
(Left foot front)

Fifth Position
(Right foot front)

Third Position
(Right foot front)

Fifth Position
(left foot front)

Second Position

Fourth
Position
(Right foot front)

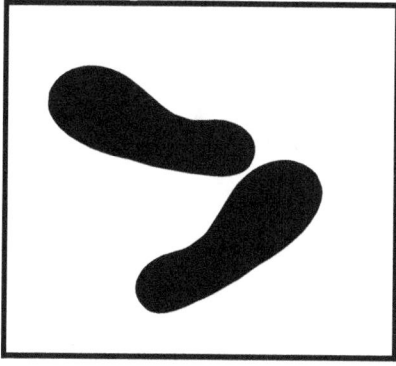

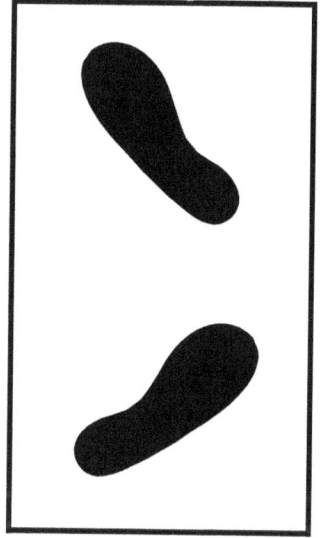

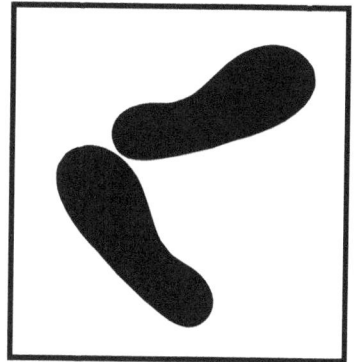

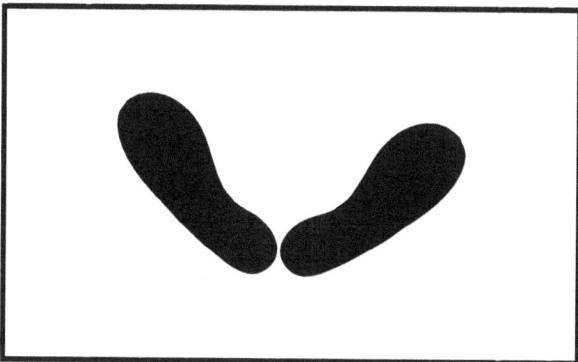

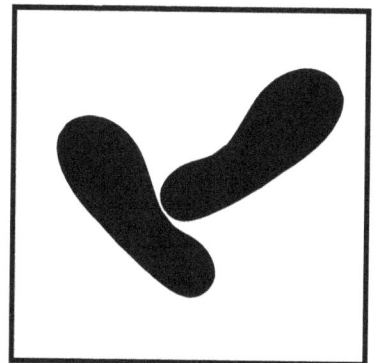

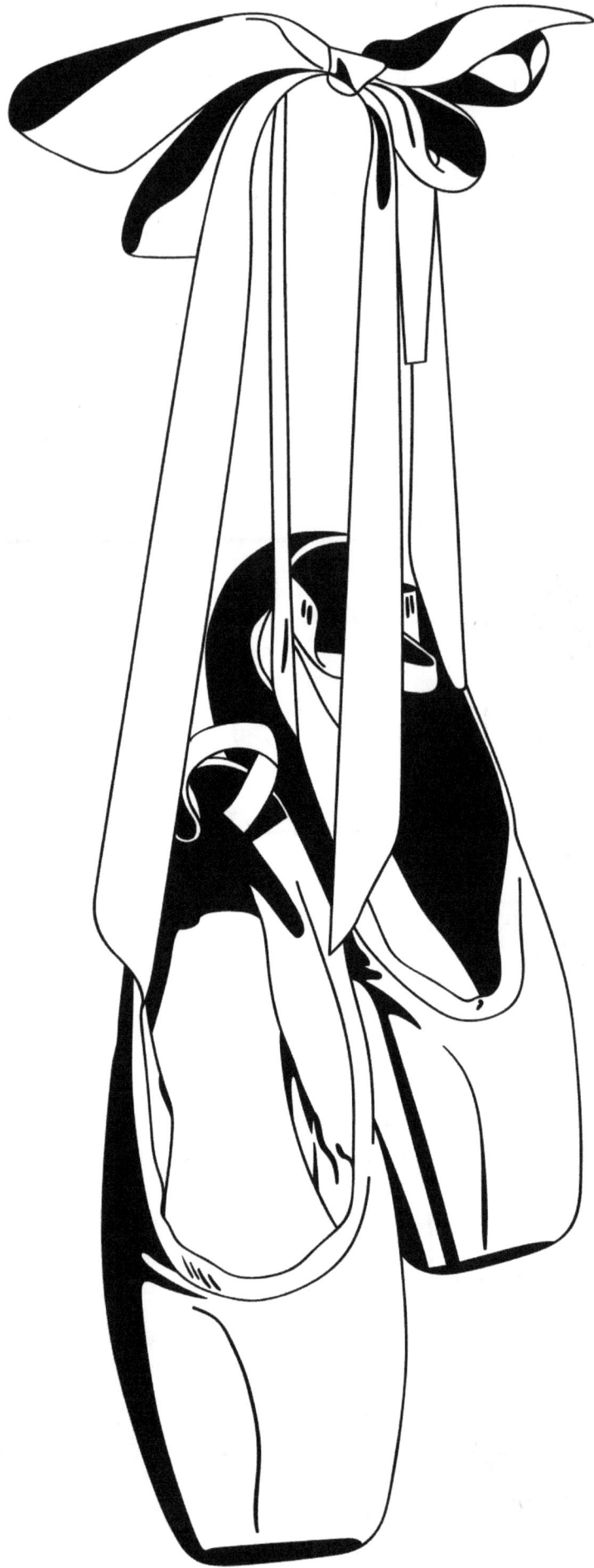

# WHY WALK WHEN YOU CAN DANCE?

# BALLET CORNERS OF THE ROOM

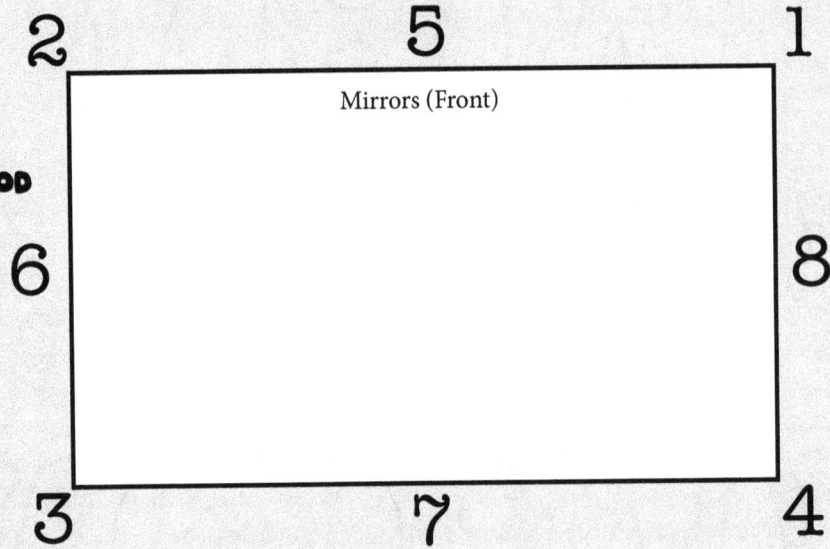

**CECCHETTI METHOD**

```
2            5            1
   ┌──────────────────────┐
   │   Mirrors (Front)    │
   │                      │
 6 │                      │ 8
   │                      │
   │                      │
   └──────────────────────┘
3            7            4
```

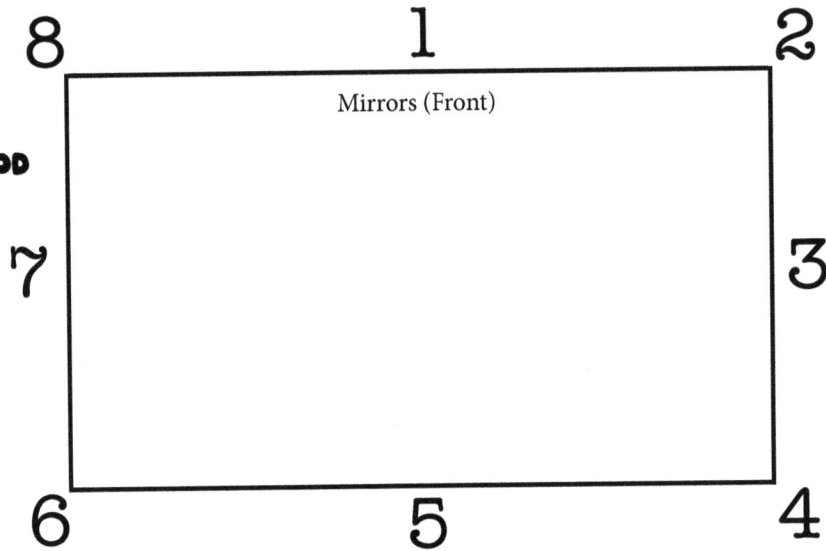

**VAGONOVA METHOD**

```
8            1            2
   ┌──────────────────────┐
   │   Mirrors (Front)    │
   │                      │
 7 │                      │ 3
   │                      │
   │                      │
   └──────────────────────┘
6            5            4
```

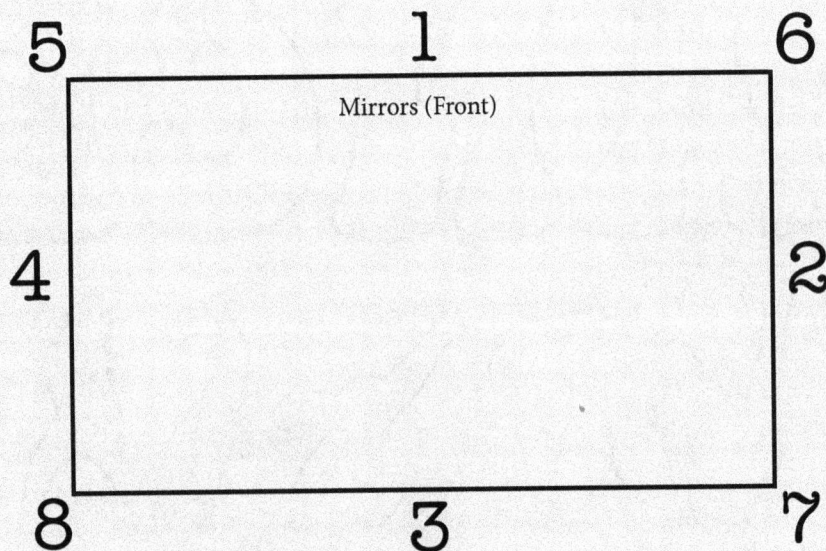

**RAD METHOD**

```
5            1            6
   ┌──────────────────────┐
   │   Mirrors (Front)    │
   │                      │
 4 │                      │ 2
   │                      │
   │                      │
   └──────────────────────┘
8            3            7
```

# LABEL THE CORNERS THAT YOU USE!

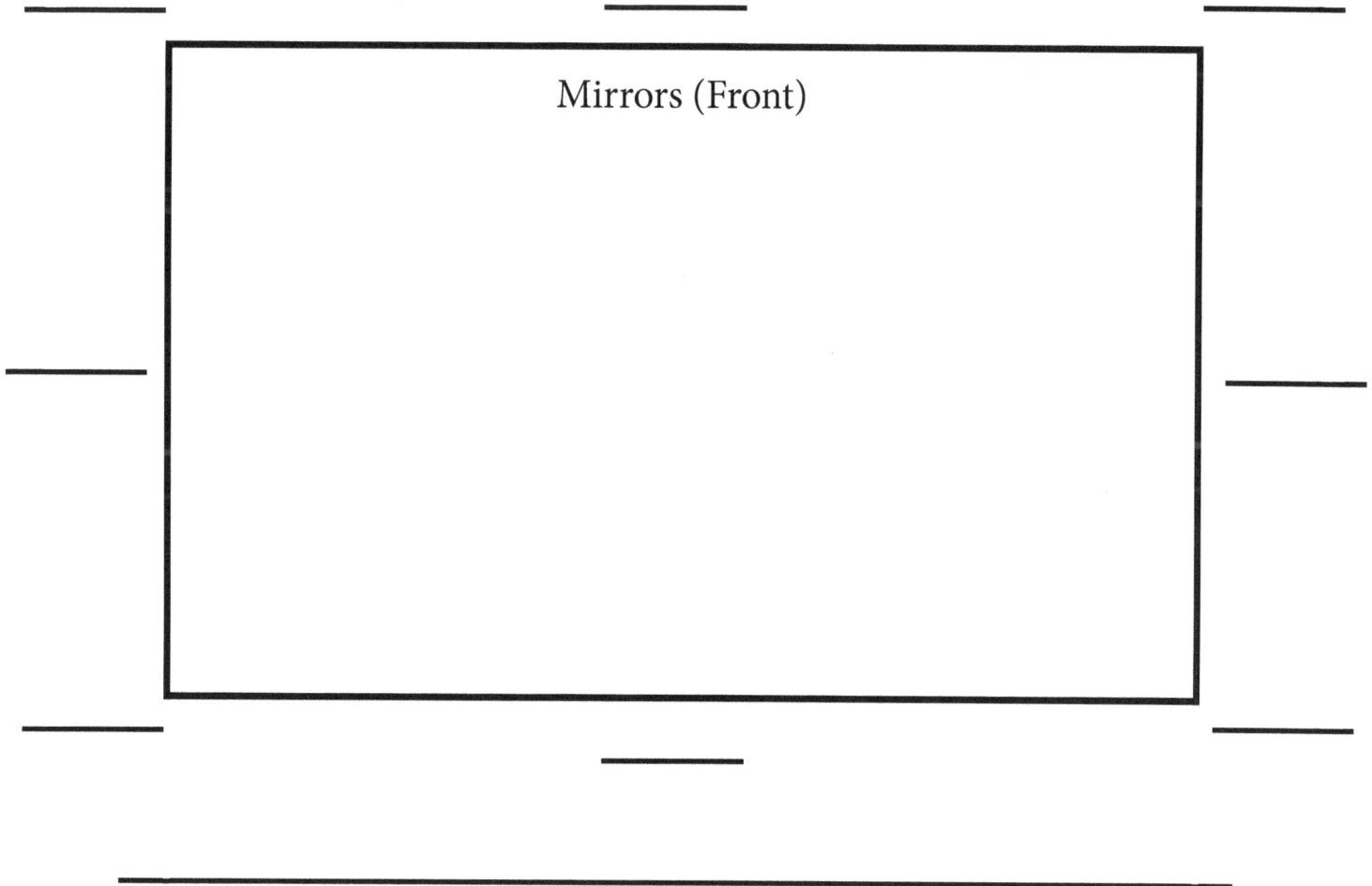

_____          _____          _____

| Mirrors (Front) |

_____                                    _____

_____          _____          _____

_____

# I LOVE TO TAP!

# LIFE IS BETTER WHEN YOU DANCE!

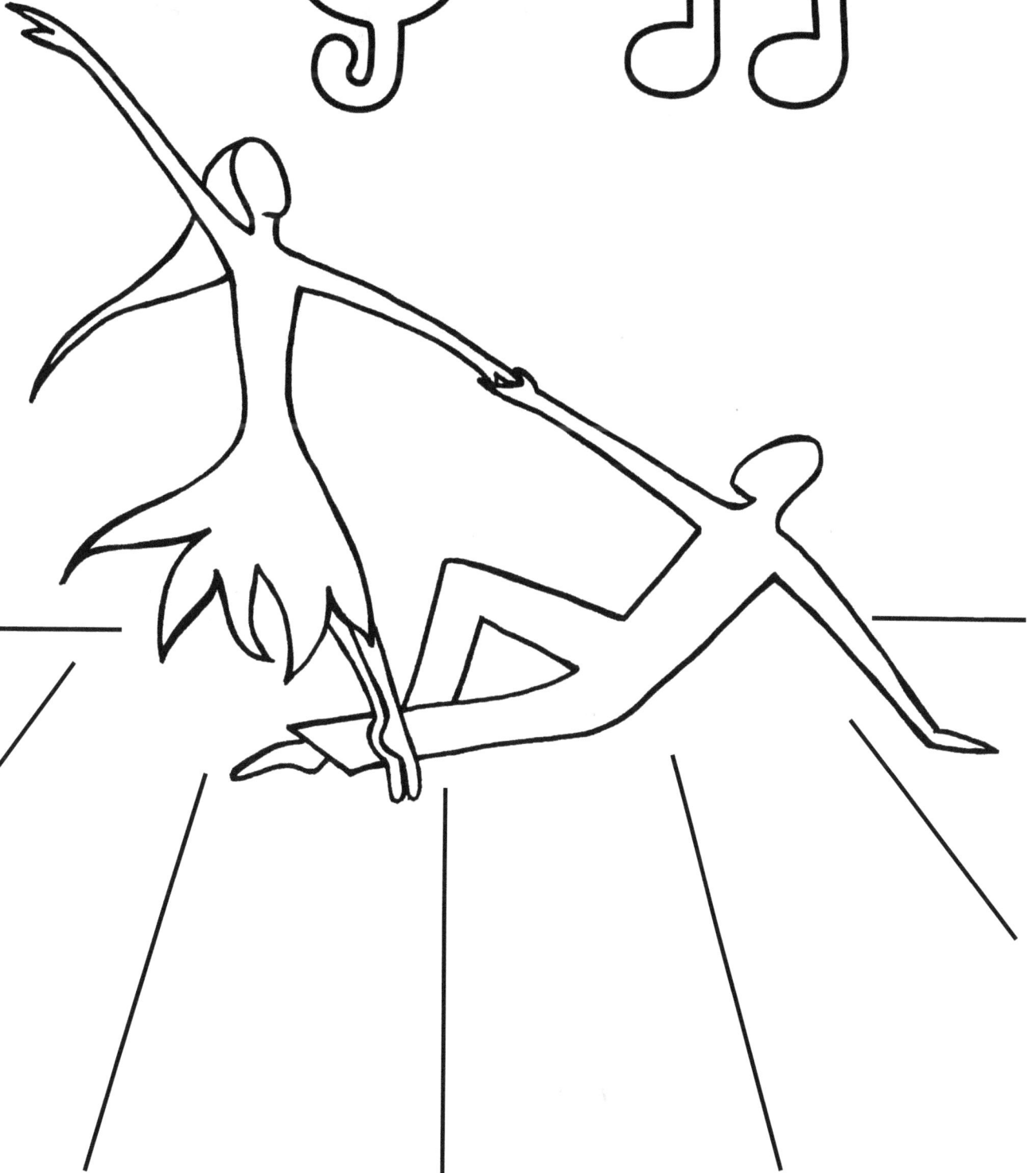

# I LOVE JAZZ DANCE!

32

# JAZZ DANCE

# BREAKDANCE!

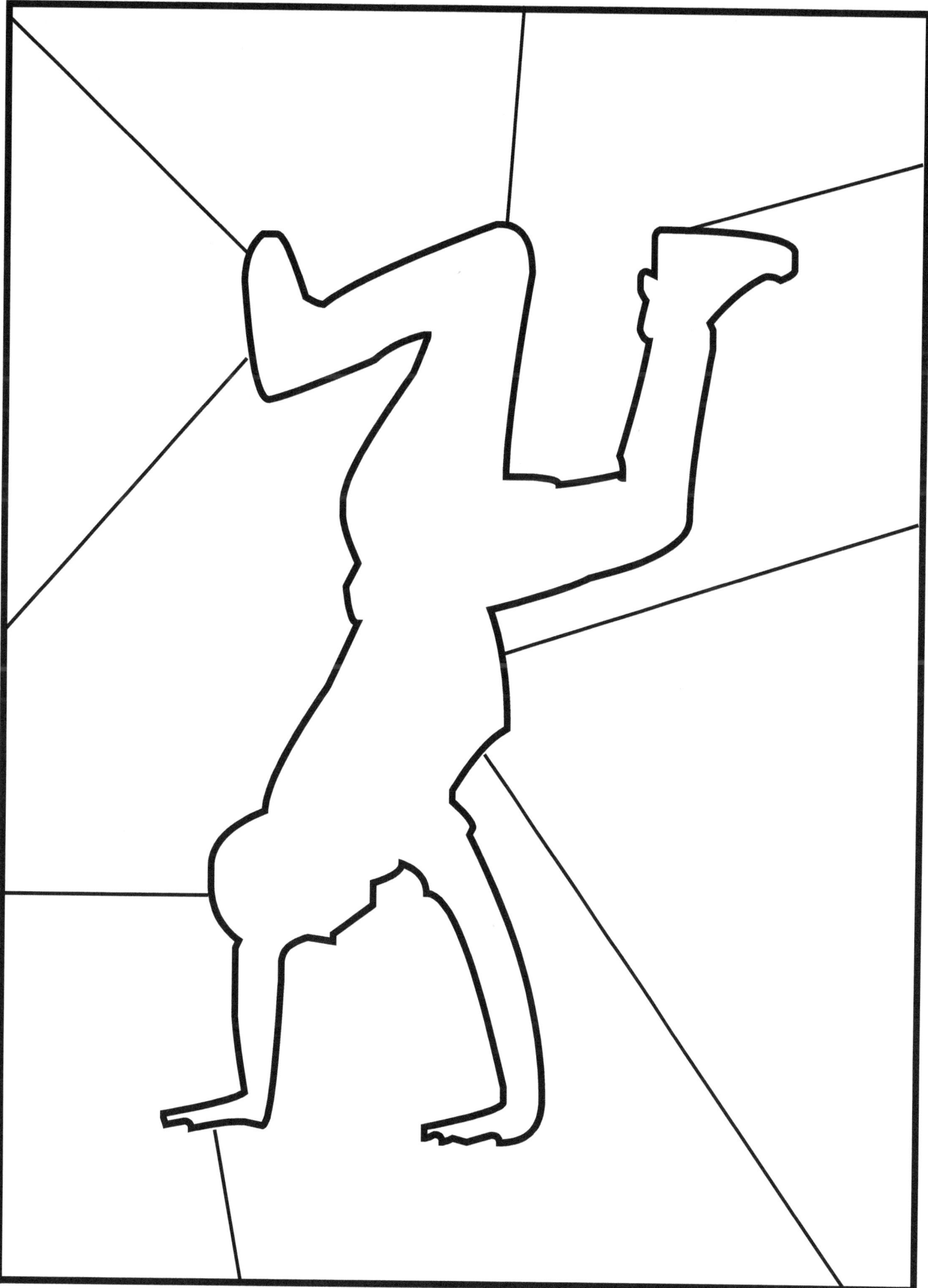

# WHEN IN DOUBT, DANCE IT OUT

# Dance to your own rhythm!

# I LOVE IRISH DANCE!

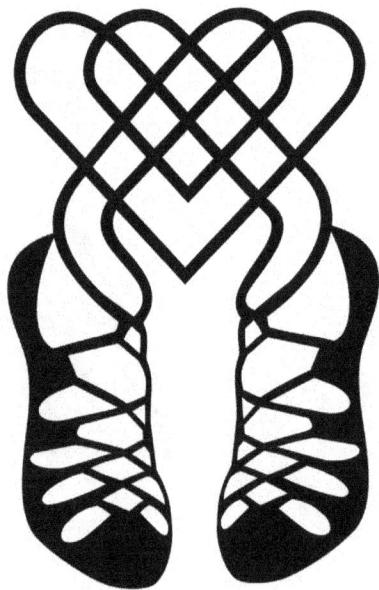

# DESIGN YOUR IRISH DANCE DRESS!

# DANCE YOUR HEART OUT!

41

I ♥

# LOVE MODERN DANCE!

♥

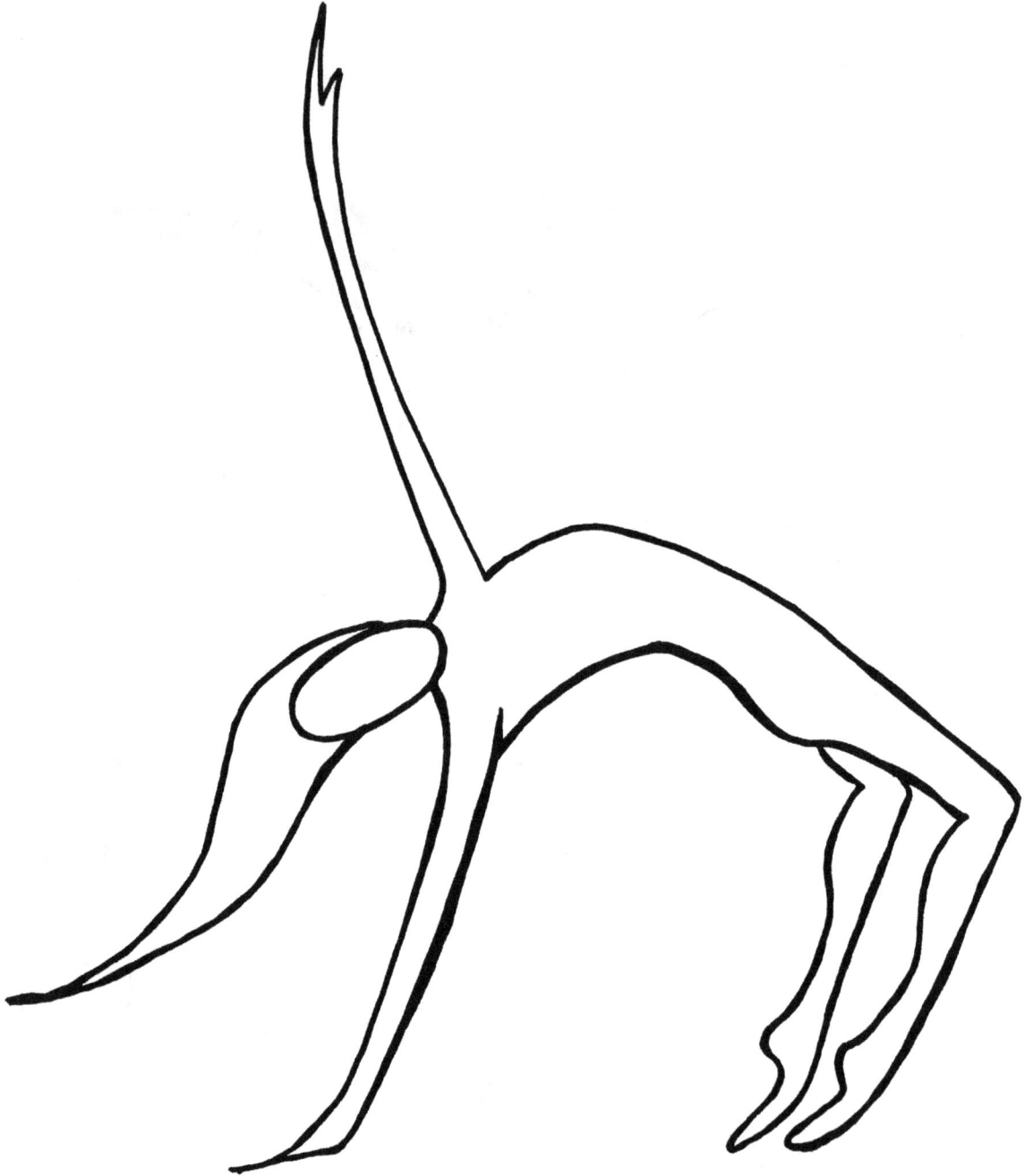

44

# DANCE IS AN ART

# KEEP CALM AND DANCE!

# TAKE MORE CHANCES, DANCE MORE DANCES!

# THE PARTS OF THE STAGE

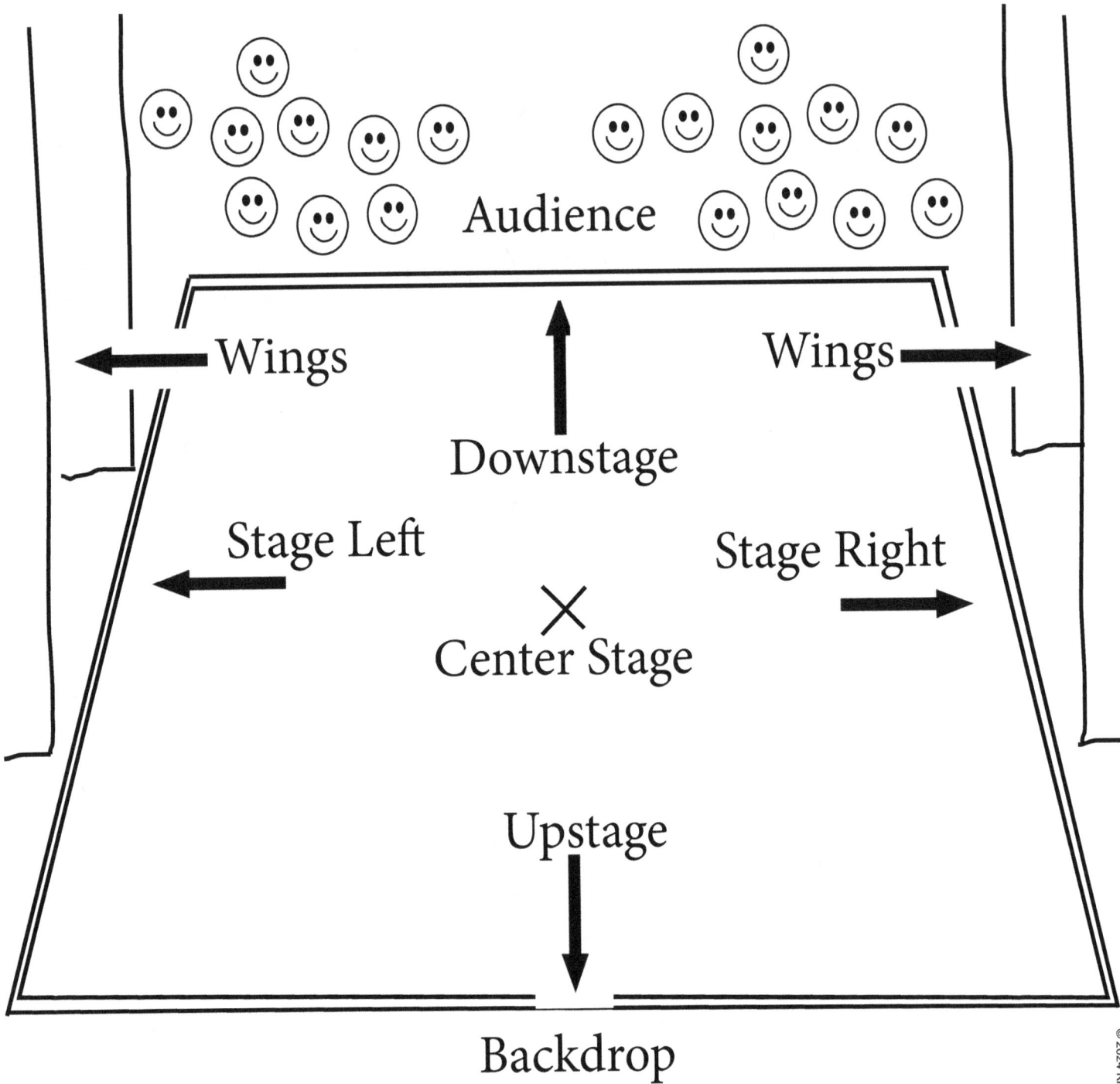

Audience

Wings ←

Wings →

↑ Downstage

Stage Left ←

Stage Right →

✕ Center Stage

Upstage ↓

Backdrop

# LABEL THE PARTS OF THE STAGE

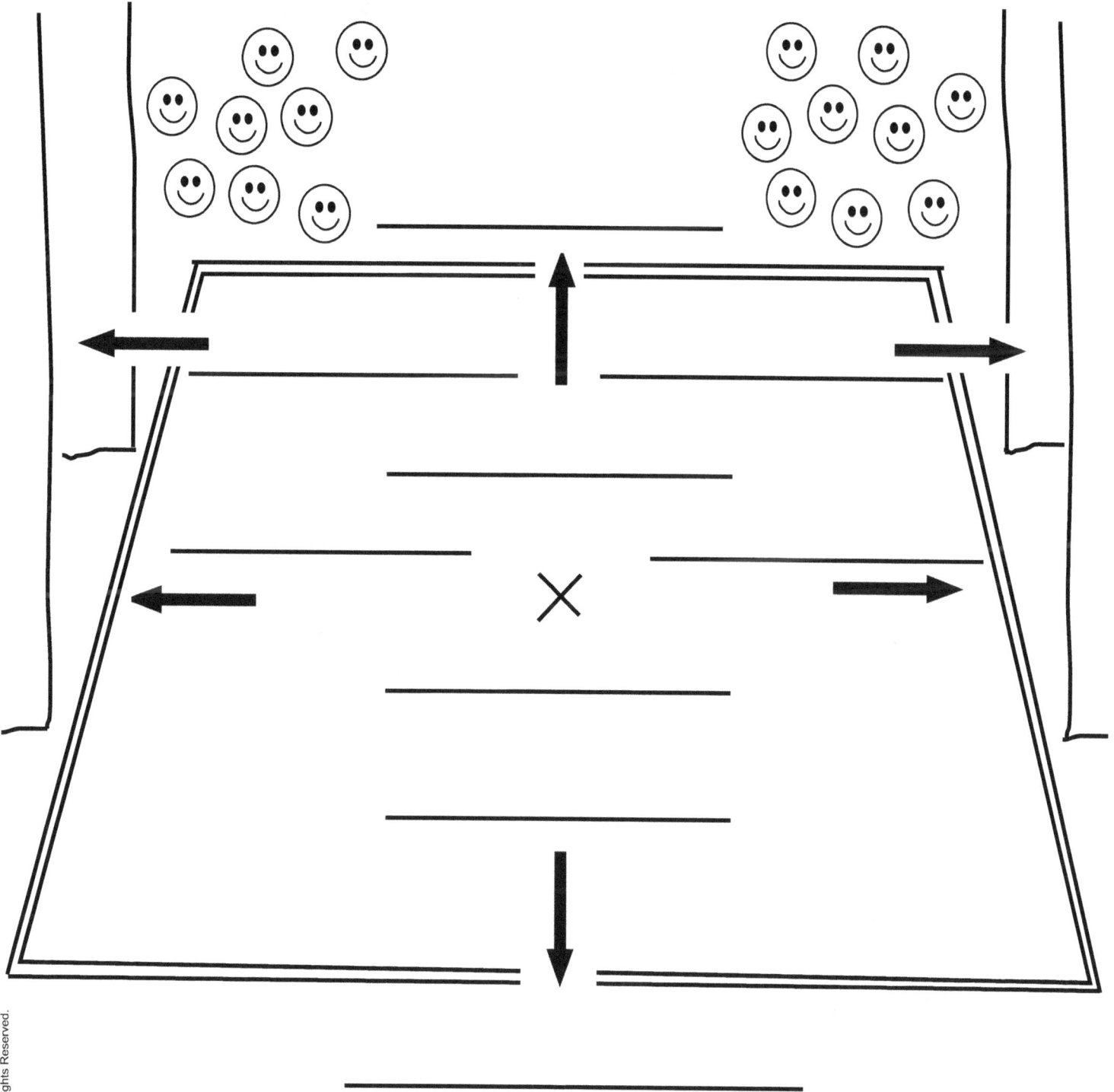

# DRAW YOUR RECITAL!

# DRAW YOUR RECITAL!

# MY RECITAL DANCE(S)

## THE SONG(S):

_____

_____

## STYLE(S) OF DANCE:

_____

_____

## THE COSTUME(S):

_____

_____

# WHAT I LEARNED IN DANCE THIS YEAR:

_____

_____

_____

_____

_____

_____

_____

_____

_____

# WHAT I WANT TO LEARN IN DANCE NEXT YEAR:

_____

_____

_____

_____

_____

_____

_____

_____

# MY FAVORITE DANCE MEMORIES:

www.ingramcontent.com/pod-product-compliance
Lightning Source LLC
Chambersburg PA
CBHW081302040426
42452CB00014B/2620